ALLENDALE TOWN

A history in photographs of a leadmining and farming community 1874 - 1934

Selected and annotated by Nora I Handcock

INTRODUCTION

The Parish of East Allendale lies in the south-west corner of Northumberland and is part of the North Pennines. Approximately twelve miles from north to south and five miles from east to west, it ascends from 200 metres at Allendale to 673 metres at Killhope Law on its southern boundary, south-west of Allenheads. The River East Allen starts its winding course above Allenheads and passes northwards through beautiful moorland scenery meeting the River West Allen at Whitfield and then flowing into the South Tyne near Ridley Hall.

Allendale was known as Allenton until 1700 when it became Allendale Town to distinguish it from the rest of the dale. The "Town" has recently been deleted from the postmarks as there is now a smaller population and no longer a market day, and it is usually referred to as a "village".

In 1861, when lead mining was at its peak, there were 6,400 people in the dale, but by 1991 there were only 1,901 in East Allendale and 220 in West Allen. In 1608 the Parish was divided into grieveships — High Forest, Low Forest, Park, Keenley, Allenton, Catton and Broadside. These came under the jurisdiction of the Archbishops of York who appointed bailiffs to have day-to-day control of local affairs. Each grieveship had its own jury of between twelve and fifteen men who appointed constables and surveyors annually, and in rotation. This was early democracy in this part of Hexhamshire, but it was a lawless area. Along with other border counties the land was ravaged and plundered and continually at war with its Scottish neighbours. Plague was rife in the middle of the 14th century and this claimed many lives, as did poverty and famine, causing depopulation. Fighting continued as a way of life throughout the Wars of the Roses 1455-1485, and the Battle of Hexham Levels in 1463.

In 1515, when Lord Dacre was Bailiff, freebooters came raiding in Allendale and burnt the Old Town driving off the cattle and carrying away plunder. Hexham Priory became the property of the Crown after the dissolution of the monasteries in 1537 and Sir Reginald Carnaby was the Bailiff for Henry VIII and also responsible to the Archbishop of York for the remaining Church properties. In 1545 the Regality of Hexham was removed from the jurisdiction of York and taken over by Henry VIII. A survey was undertaken to assess the value of the properties for rents. Names of the copyholders and their property were recorded and similar names exist today but with spelling variations. There were 40 tenancies in 1547 and by the next survey in 1608 this number had doubled. A gallows was erected in 'Alwentdale' in 1662 also the stocks, which remained until 1810. The Market cross was removed in 1840, Allendale having been granted a Charter in the reign of Edward I to hold markets. Life though hard, was relatively peaceful after the Union of Scotland and England under James I until the 1715 uprising. The curate of Allendale, Robert Paton, joined the Jacobite forces and was appointed chaplain under General Forster in support of the ill fated Earl of Derwentwater and Bonnie Prince Charlie. Paton survived only by turning

King's evidence and later he wrote the History of the Late Rebellion. Rebel Hill near Catton is reputed to be the rallying-place of the troopers. Paton was released from prison but never returned to Allendale and ended his days in Cumbria. George Fox the Quaker preached in Allendale around 1660. The movement gained strength in spite of much persecution and a Meeting House of the Society of Friends was built at Limestone Brae in West Allen. A year later another was built at the Burnfoot on land belonging to Francis Shield. The present Meeting House was rebuilt in 1868 and is still in use.

Methodism, i.e. Wesleyanism, was introduced by Christopher Hopper, an itinerant preacher and schoolmaster from Ryton, in 1747. John Wesley visited Hindley Hill in 1748 and 1749. He also preached in Allendale. The first chapel was built at Keenley in 1750. Over the next sixty years every hamlet had its own chapel. After 1827 Primitive Methodists started by Thomas Batty in Allendale built the chapels for the workers and miners and "less privileged" dalesfolk. Altogether there were 23 stone buildings for worship in East and West Allen. Today seven Methodist and two Anglican churches remain.

Many buildings can be dated from the late 18th century but they have been altered and extended as farming changed and families increased. Those which are difficult to reach have fallen into decay and can be seen only by walkers.

The history of leadmining has been well documented and this former industry has left many sites of archaeological interest over the moors, and in Allenheads village. The first part of this century was one of modernisation and expansion for holiday makers who were escaping to the country for good farmfare and healthy climate. Evacuation from wars brought more townsfolk.

There was no main sewerage until 1927 and no electricity until 1937 but some benefits came from the rail service to Catton built in 1867 and new houses were built along Station Road. A bus service in 1929 meant loss of rail passenger traffic so the line closed, except for goods, in 1930, and was finally shut down altogether in 1950. Telephone boxes were put in the dale in 1927. The 'Bull Ring' was removed in 1927. The chains round the village green went for salvage in 1942. The lych gate erected in 1920 as a War Memorial, had 22 names inscribed on it, and two more men were killed in the 1939-45 war. The village was no longer the same.

The illustrations in this book tell some of the history of the 'Toon' as it was in the early days of photography and the era when picture postcards started to be fashionable. Many cannot be included because space is limited but perhaps other hamlets in the dale will be included in future publications.

Dates of some photographs are approximate but as near as possible.

ACKNOWLEDGEMENTS

I am very grateful to all those residents of Allendale who have generously loaned or given me old photographs for reproduction. It is not possible to include all items in this book but they will nevertheless provide a valuable record for the archives.

In particular I am indebted to Mrs H Makepeace, Mrs R Lindsay, Mrs E Edgar, Mrs J Bell, Mrs E Fairless, Mrs D Lowery, Mrs J Walker and the late Mrs N Fairlamb; Mr C W Harrison, Mr F Nattrass, Mr A Smith, Mr T Shield, Mr J Hutchinson, Mr J Glenwright and the late Mr J Stephenson for historical information. The photographs on pages 11 and 21 are reproduced by permission of the University of Newcastle upon Tyne; those on pages 36 and 46 by permission of Beamish, North of England Open Air Museum; the aerial view on the inside back cover by permission of Aerofilms Ltd.

I would like to thank also Northumberland County Library and County Record Office staff for their help and interest in making this publication possible.

Allendale railway station in 1905. The railway was opened for goods traffic in 1867 and for passengers in 1869. It ended at Catton, but was originally designed to go to Allenheads. The Hexham and Allendale Railway Company sold out to the North-Eastern Railway Company in 1876. The line was closed for passenger traffic in 1930 but carried goods until its closure in November 1950. Thomas Douglas was the last Station Master.

This three-horse brake belonged to the Forster family who lived in West View, the house to the left on the cover picture. It would meet people at the station and take them up the dale.

On the way they would come along Station Road or the New Line as it is sometimes called. This was a turnpike road made in 1845. Across the fields were the remains of Beaumont's Smelt Mill. Most of the local population were connected with the lead industry until this was closed in 1897.

Leadgate had a toll gate and a gatehouse on the right, which was built by the Alston Turnpike Trust in 1827 and removed in 1878 when the Highway Board took over. It was opposite the Temperance Hall — now a garden.

LEADGATE ROAD   ALLENDALE

823

Leadgate c.1918, showing the Temperance Hall built in 1905 and mothers waiting outside school for their children. The fountain was erected in 1903 in memory of Trooper John J Glendinning who was killed in the South African war. It replaced one of the traditional water pumps, some of which can still be seen in the village today.

Allendale Board School was opened in April 1880 for infants. Its first headmaster was Emerson Peart. It is now a First School for pupils from five to nine years of age. Senior children remained at Brides Hill School, built in 1851 by Mr Beaumont, but it closed in 1887 and an extension was added to the Board School.

The Old Thatched Cottage ('Thacky') was last occupied by John Ridley a cobbler. Unfortunately it was allowed to decay and fell apart in the early 1950s. Its heather thatch and high pitched roof was typical of early dwellings in the dale. There was an old oven built on the outside wall. In the background are the Savings Bank built in 1875 and the second Primitive Methodist Church built on the site of old cottages in 1878 and adjacent to its 1833 predecessor (now the Scout Hall).

1903 view looking south towards Heatherlea Hotel still with scaffolding (see p.30). The building on the right was a wheelwright's shop, and on the left was the Police House.

THE OLD JOINERS SHOP OLD ALLENDALE

A close-up view of the 'Cart and Carriage Builders'. Unfortunately the roof was destroyed by fire on 11 December 1900 but the joiner, John W Glenwright, continued with the glazing and woodwork for Catton Church which was completed by January 1902. Lambton's Bank was built on the site of the ruined shop in 1904. The Parish complained that it encroached on a portion of land "used by the public for the last 50 years". Lloyds took over the bank in 1909.

School children seem intrigued with the photographer or are they on a visit to the Savings Bank on the right? It was erected on the site of the old candle making factory. The large building at the back is the Industrial and Provident Society, founded in 1874 and later called the Co-operative Society.

A similar view shows the Lion House Hotel enlarged in 1839, and on the left the King's Head, the oldest inn in Allendale dating from c.1776.

This shop, now called Victoria House, stood on the site of the former Three Tuns Inn. The licensee moved to the Golden Lion in 1863 and David Edgar built this house and shop. He and his wife Mary had six boys and seven girls. This photo, c.1880, shows six of the youngest children. Herbert (born 1864) took over the shop, a grocers and drapers, about 1900.

The post brake outside the King's Head. John S Shield left Allenheads at 7 am arrived here at 8.15 am went to Catton station to collect mail and returned to Allenheads at 11 am — a round trip of 16 miles which he repeated from 5 pm to 8.45 pm. Not a very pleasant trip in the winter, on rough roads.

On the same side of the square in 1875 there was a Temperance Hotel, not a very attractive one, but it was needed to counteract the excessive number of public houses, and a brewery — Wilson's Lee & Co., once situated near The Riding. In 1886 Joseph Forster was the proprietor, (see p 19).

Allendale. 2195

Joseph Forster's family lived in West View after 1915. Daughters Isabella and Mary Jane became the proprietors of the Temperance Hotel. The building was modernised and the roof raised. The two cottages and butcher's shop on the left were pulled down. A pair of semi-detached houses replaced them in 1932. The first Co-op Store was in the building adjacent to the hotel along the lane. It was founded in 1874. There was a bank and a saddlers in the left hand house, adjoining Forsters.

ALLENDALE

The second Co-op, seen in the centre, was here c.1875. The first Manager was John James Allison (1845-1915). A Primitive Methodist preacher, Parish Council Chairman and School Manager he was "beloved and trusted by the community". His house, which was part of the shop, was originally called Curtain House, then West View. On the right is J R Stephenson's. He was a grocer, greengrocer and collector of income tax.

Allendale Post Office started in 1870 near the old Candle House but was pulled down before 1875. William Fairlamb moved to these premises as a Stationers and Newsagent. He was also the Emigration Agent and Royal Exchange Fire Assurance agent. He sold cement, fire bricks, kitchen ranges and cream separators. His son Llewellyn was postmaster and telegraph officer from 1904. In 1953 Llewellyn's son William and wife Nancy took over the shop on the right, once a joiners, then Knights Bakers, and converted it into the Post Office. William retired in 1970.

A close-up view of the Co-op shop. The lady and gentleman in the gig are bedecked for a Royal event, so is the house. It was probably the Coronation of King Edward VII on 9 August 1902.

DALE HOUSE + KINGS HEAD HOTELS ALLENDALE

The Dale Hotel after 1920 was run by Connie and Mrs Margaret Simpson and William. After 1925, Connie married Arcus Thompson and continued as pro-prietress. William married Laura Edgar and bought Deneholme as a private hotel in December 1933. Mary Jane and Isabella Forster had retired from the Dale in 1920 to West View the centre house in this picture and the Co-op shopfront was removed. It was pulled down in 1936 to make way for the new Co-op Drapery, the Forsters went to Victoria House.

This 1807 church had a new tower added but it was not as high as intended "owing to the failure of the contractor during its erection". A large new bell was hung in 1815.

In 1873 alterations were again necessary and the tower was raised to its intended height, also the roof of the nave. The Rector, Rev. Titus Emerson, died before it was completed. There is a stained glass window to his memory as well as other interesting memorials. The Sunday School was built in 1879 on the site of some old cottages in Huntington Place and extended in 1891. The clock was erected in 1906. This 1904 card does not show the Lych Gate that is here today. It covers the entrance and was erected as a Memorial to the First World War in 1920. From 1940 until 1958 the Sunday School room was a cinema.

The Smithy, Allendale

Gibson & Son, Hexham.

164

This card probably dates from 1900. The building was erected by blacksmith Thomas Iley who married Elizabeth White in 1740. Their first son Thomas was baptised in 1747. On a headstone above the door were the initials T & E I 1747, also G & S A 1883, probably George and Sarah Arnison who owned the property at that time. There is a car showroom on the site today.

The blacksmith seen shoeing the horse c.1920 was William Hutchinson with his son Jack, watching. The men in the doorway were Isaac Dixon the butcher, and Matthew Maughan, farmer.

This was taken **before** 1875 as it shows the second Wesleyan Chapel built in 1839 (the original being 1760). The present Methodist building had its foundation stone laid in October 1875.

Shield Street in 1875. The white house was an ale house. More recently it was the caretaker's cottage for the Wesleyan Methodist church next door. Now it is a private house.

Heatherlea Hotel c.1905. The trees were planted in 1897 to commemorate Queen Victoria's Diamond Jubilee. "Three Sycamore trees and ten shrubs were planted in the centre of Allendale town within an iron railing which had been fixed a few days before to enclose them" — Dickinson. The "Bull Ring" as it was known, was dismantled in 1927.

Before Heatherlea was built Matthew Stephenson had a General Dealers shop. At the back of the premises i.e. behind the Allendale Hotel, were Stephenson & Bell's livery stables. The Cumberland Union Bank was in the corner of the building. It was taken over by the Midland Bank which moved to the new premises in 1927 and closed in 1992.

George Short was a fruiterer and saddler in 1902. This shop, now a hairdressing salon, has had a variety of uses. In 1909 it was a butchers. Isaac Dixon had it until the Co-op butchery was built in 1927. In 1900 in Shield Street there was T W Hall ironmongers, J A Edgar fruiterer and florist, P Hetherington cabinet maker and wood carver and W E Dickinson chemist, who was also Deputy Registrar and Clerk to the school board. A George Short of Bridge End drove the Co-op carts, could this be him?

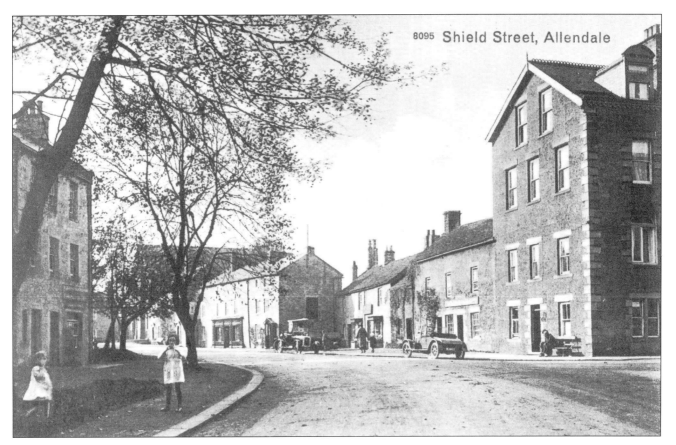

8095 Shield Street, Allendale

Shield Street in the early 1930s. From right to left there was Heatherlea Hotel, H Noble's cobbler's shop, Charlton's grocery store and H Blake MPS Pharmacist. On the opposite side of the road there was a drapers — Annie Nora Bell, and Miss Hipson's a fruiterer and market gardeners (Shields brothers had it as a cycle shop later). These are now private houses.

A BIT OF OLD ALLENDALE IN 1876

This was referred to as the 'High Street' in the 1891 census, Arnison Terrace was a later name, a tribute to the doctor of that name. His family owned the cottages and the fields behind. They had been surgeons for three generations in Allendale from 1794 to 1904 and lived in Selah House (now The Hotspur Hotel). The white building was the Rose and Crown Inn. The shop was John Forster's which sold linen and woollen goods. George Dodd and his wife had a shop here with a fish and chip shop at the rear, after the last war.

Elizabeth Bell and her brother Abraham outside the ancient Rose and Crown. A sister, Hannah, married Llewellyn Fairlamb from the Post Office in 1899 and united two very large well-known Dale families. The inn changed its name to The Old Oaks.

This lovely old house called Woodbine House was lived in by Thomas and sister Hannah Bushby. After Hannah died in 1903, it was used as a doctor's surgery by Dr. Murray. It was converted into the Midland Bank in 1927 and was in business until its closure in 1992.

LONKLEY HILL FROM ALLENDALE

1656

This later postcard shows the Midland Bank c.1928 before the bungalow was built on the corner of Lonkley (called Morland). The first Midland Bank took over the Cumberland Union Bank. This was on the corner of Heatherlea and the agent was Matthew Stephenson a grocer who at that time had the shop. (See p. 31).

Allendale Bridge.

Gibson & Son, Hexham, No. 188

This postcard stamped 1904 shows the steep bank to the River Allen. The bridge had the largest single span in the County. It was built in 1825 to replace the Bow Bridge which was narrow with recesses in the side. This one had to be strengthened a few years ago to take the weight of modern vehicles.

A mill race carried water to a wheel on the far side of this corn mill and thence into a tunnel under the road into the River Allen. A survey made by the Archbishop of York for Henry VIII records "In 1547 Hugh Shield held a water cornemill in Est Alwent" and is believed to refer to this site. The little cottage in the bottom corner was a toll gate house, one of three controlling entry into the town until 1875.

The farmers brought their barley or oats to be ground at A & G Little's corn mill. The weather was often unsuitable for cereal growing and the soil too wet so grain was bought in. The Mill sold cattle feedstuffs. The workers in this group have not been identified, the lady on the horse is Miss Vida Telfer (later Mrs Norman Walton) from Haydon Bridge.

Also at Bridge End is this lovely Georgian house, shown c.1900, built by Ralph Reed of Haydon Bridge in 1839 for William Harrison his brother in law, who retired in 1840 as the manager of the Bridge End Mill. It is still in the Harrison family. Maria Metcalf sold sweets — black bullets, tobacco and paraffin.

This must be the oldest photograph in the book. Dickinson wrote in 1900 "October 1860, the 7th Northumberland (Allendale) Rifle Volunteer Corps was established. The first officers were Captain Sopwith, Lieutenant Coats, Ensign George Arnison and Drill Sergeant Wood". Later this was the 1st Volunteer F Brigade Northumberland Fusiliers who held mock battles around the town. The parade is lined up across the Store Bank outside the joiners shop. Note the remains of the village pound on the left.

Also on Store Bank was J W Robson's Central Store. It was a new extended building — compare with the earlier photograph. His shop had a fire in 1910. He lived at the bottom of Lonkley in Morland built by Nichol Glendinning c.1930. His daughter Lena was manageress in the Co-op Drapery.

A group of motor cycle enthusiasts in 1913 at the rear of the King's Head Inn. The lady is Miss Weatheritt, better known as Mrs Rood in later years. Wilfred Allison (a teacher at Allendale and Lowgate), Norman Allison (killed in the First World War) and John G Nevin (a Councillor for 54 years Parish, District and County. He served the community in many spheres and farmed at Parkside) are 4th, 5th and 6th from the left respectively. Others are not known.

1925. A day out in the country by charabanc — "The Dalesman" — a bright yellow Napier. The driver, second on the left, is Fred Handcock who with his brother Alfred were Motor Engineers at Allen Mill, Ethel Shield is sitting centre back.

Laying the Foundation stone of the Temperance Hall, now renamed the Village Hall, on Whit Monday, 15 June 1905. Many people came by train, pony and trap or on foot for this event, organised by the British Women's Temperance Association. They took two years to raise £400 towards the £900 needed. The building was completed for the opening on 7 October 1905. The joiners were Messrs Lowe of Thornley Gate and P Hetherington of Cross Keys, the mason was F Charlton of The Spital.

May Day Fete 1908 — Outside the Temperance Hall. Tom Brown, Willy Edgar (in doorway); Miss Elliot and Miss Annie Dickinson (Stephenson) — teachers; Back Row L to R:— Not known, Eddie Fairless, Amy Glendinning, Roland Bell, ?? White, Sallie Charlton, Cecil Hetherington, Maggie Glendinning, Jack Stephenson. Right 2nd half row:— Barbara Scott, Percy Edgar, George Maughan, Billy Brown (in Tartan). Middle Row:— Maud Graham, Sally Reed, Edith Shortridge, Annie Bell, Florrie Payne, Olive Rodmell, Ethel Bell, Maggie Keen, Boy in cocked hat ?? Front Row:— May Bell and Emmy Bell — sisters, Katy Bell, Frances Fairless, Nellie Fairlamb, Annie Fairlamb.

New Year's Eve c.1970. From L to R:— Clive Bell, Fred Fairless, Joseph H Bell (1909-1982) joiner and undertaker in Allendale all his life, he carried a tar barrel every New Year as his father Lancelot also had done for many years, ??, Lawrence Smith. This ancient tradition is carried out by forty men in fancy dress. The 'Guisers' as they are called, parade round the village with their flaming tar 'barls' on their heads, to the band's accompaniment of traditional tunes like The White Cockade and The Keel Row. They toss their barrels onto the fire at midnight with 'Auld Lang Syne' echoing round the square. 'Happy New Year' greetings to one and all!